Published in the United States of America by Tommy Starling.
www.bobtheladybug.com
Library of Congress Catalog Card Number: 2012912725
ISBN 978–0615668482
First Edition July 2012

BOB
THE LADYBUG
Bob's New Pants

Written By Tommy Starling

Illustrated by Jacquie Gonzalez

Acknowledgements

To my friend and illustrator, Jacquie Gonzalez, THANK YOU for your beautiful soul and magical illustrations. You brought Bob to life.

Special thanks to Jonathan Parfitt, a very talented graphic designer, who assisted in the illustration and design of the characters in Bob the Ladybug.

Very Special Thank you to my dear friend, Will Halm for his major support of the book and my endeavors.

Special Thanks to my friends that helped Bob grow his wings:
Mark MacDougal
Kevin S Montgomery
Damon Wolf
Sonny Ward
Carl Valloric
Greta Snakelady Patterson
Zuni Johnson

To my husband, Jeff Littlefield, thank you for giving me strength and courage and for making my journey through life more meaningful.

This book is dedicated to my daughter, Carrigan Shea Starling-Littlefield. You are my reason for waking up every morning. Daddy is trying to make the world a better place for you. I love you.

For Carrigan...

This is a story about a ladybug named Bob. Bob lives in a big, yellow dandelion in a colorful backyard garden in the fragrant town of Floraville.

Bob's home grows just below a small patch of tulips, under a beautiful, red rosebush. In YOUR backyard or park, see if you can find Bob sometime!

Bob lives with his mom, Edna, his dad, Tom, and his little sister, Lilly.

BOB'S FAMILY

Bob is a quiet, shy, and friendly ladybug.
He has a disctinct, white spot on his back
that sets him apart from other ladybugs.
He spends most of his days flying
around Floraville exploring new things.
Bob is very curious, and he loves to learn.

One Day, Bob was leaving home in another beautiful dress his mom made for him, but today for some reason, Bob felt uncomfortable. "Mom, why do I always wear dresses?" he asked. "You're a ladybug," his mom replied. "Your dad wears a dress...ladybugs wear dresses." Bob never wanted to disappoint his mother, so he went out to play in the pink and white striped dress.

"Hi Bob," yelled Shea, Bob's best friend in all of Floraville. "What a pretty dress you are wearing! Wouldn't it look better on a cute girl like me?" Shea asked. Bob smiled at Shea but thought to himself... *I know ladybugs wear dresses, but I am a boy. Why can't I wear pants like other boy bugs?*

Bob flew home upset and confused.

He was hiding in the closet, when he cried, "Mom, I need to talk to you."

"Mom, I want to wear pants like other boy bugs." Bob's mom took a moment to think. She just wanted Bob to fit in and be like all ladybugs, but more importantly, Edna loved her son and wanted him to be happy.

"Bob, there are many kinds of bugs, and they dress in different ways. I have seen daddy long legs in dresses and bicoastal earwigs who wear earmuffs on a hot day! Being yourself and doing what makes you happy is the best way to live." said Bob's mom. She hugged him, dried his tears, and agreed he could wear pants.

Edna worked through the night sewing the perfect pair of pants.

When Bob woke up the next morning, he was so excited to show off his new pants to all of his friends. Bob had a new confidence in himself because of his stylish blue pants!

Bob went to Shea's home in the white tulip next door to his dandelion house. He had a BIG surprise. "Shea!" yelled Bob, "Look at my new blue pants!"

"Wow! They look great on you!" Shea replied. "I think you were born to wear pants!" "I think so, too," said Bob proudly. "I want you to have my dress, Shea. I think it fits you." Shea thanked Bob. She put on the dress, and they flew over to the playground.

Bob had never really noticed it before, but there *were* other ladybugs wearing pants. Some were boys and some were girls. His friends Malina, Luc, and Harley had on pants.

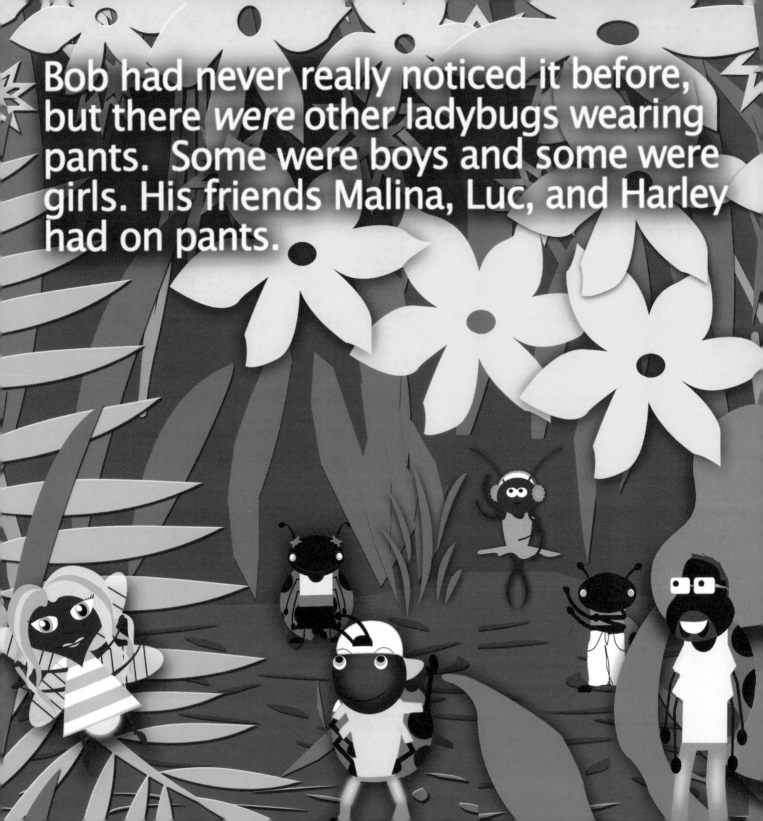

Bob also noticed Zuni, Jake, and Ada were wearing stylish short pants. Walo and Sam wore their pants proudly as they approached Bob and Shea. Bob felt great!

Just then, Ben the Bullybug jumped in front of Bob and sneered, "You look funny in those pants!" "No I don't," replied Bob, staring directly into all four of Bullybug's eyes. "There are all kinds of bugs who wear many kinds of clothes! Open *all* of your eyes *and* your mind, Ben, and you will see."

Then, Ben the Bullybug turned to notice other ladybugs in pants and daddy long legs wearing dresses. All the bugs were staring him down. Chelsea, Greta, and Sammy stood behind Bob to show their support and to stand up to Ben the Bullybug. Ben grumbled something, tucked his wings between his legs, and walked away from Bob and all of his new friends.

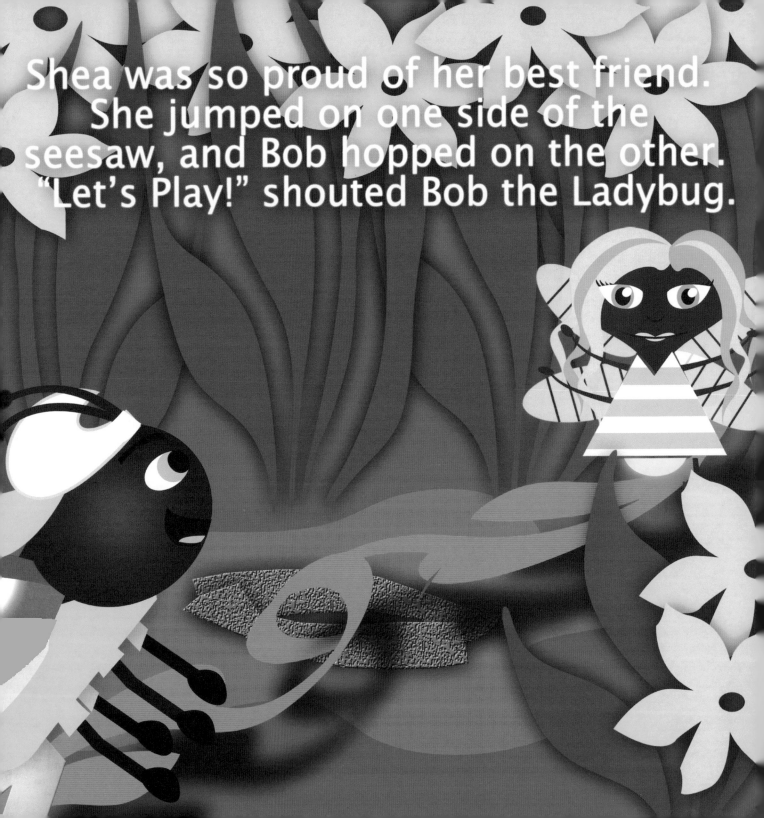

Shea was so proud of her best friend. She jumped on one side of the seesaw, and Bob hopped on the other. "Let's Play!" shouted Bob the Ladybug.

The

End

About the Author

Tommy Starling lives in Pawleys Island, SC with his husband and young daughter. He is a native of North Carolina and comes from a very conservative family. His life experiences as well as his journey to acceptance from friends and family have given him many topics to write about. Tommy is an entrepreneur and equal rights advocate who works hard to ensure children grow up with respect for everyone.

Tommy came up with the idea of Bob The Ladybug while on a trip to New Orleans. He created Bob to gain the attention of young children in an effort to teach them life lessons about mutual respect, empathy, and caring. His mission to create Bob started with a desire to improve the world around his daughter and make her life more pleasant.

Stay in touch with Bob and keep up with his other adventures at www.bobtheladybug.com.

You can also "Like" Bob on Facebook at: https://www.facebook.com/BobTheLadybug

Be on the lookout for Bob's next book!